LOVE AFTER 50

Love Questions from DearCathy.com After Hours

CATHY HARRIS

Angels Press, Austin, TX
http://www.AngelsPress.com

Published By:
Angels Press
P.O. Box 19282
Austin, TX 78760
Phone: (512) 909-7365
http://www.angelspress.com
info@angelspress.com

ATTENTION UNIVERSITIES, COLLEGES, AND PROFESSIONAL ORGANIZATIONS: Quantity discounts are available in bulk purchases of this book for educational and gift purposes. Special books or book excerpts can also be created to fit specific needs. For information, please contact Angels Press, P.O. Box 19282, Austin, TX 78760, Phone: (512) 909-7365, http://www.angelspress.com, info@angelspress.com.

Book Cover: Torrie Cooney
(http://www.TorrieCooney.com)

DEDICATION

This book is dedicated to everyone seeking to form a meaningful love relationship and build the type of life that they can truly love.

CONTENTS

Dedication   iii

Preface   vii

1   **Section I - Singles Over 50 Love Issues**   1

Still Hoping and Searching for Love   1

Dating A Younger Man   3

True Love - But Two Households   5

Mate Won't Destroy Sex Tape   6

In Love With Friend's Ex   8

New Mate Too Clingy   10

In Abusive Relationship   12

Mate is the Jealous Type   14

Dating Outside My Race   16

Bald Men Make Better Lovers   18

Getting Breast Implants for Mate   19

2   **Section II - Couples Over 50 Love Issues**   22

Sick of Being Sexless in Seattle   22

Wife Seeks More Intimacy   24

Couple Need to Shop Online   26

Husband Left Alone on New Years   27

Husband Can't Say He Loves Wife   29

Married to a Homebody   32

Senior Couple Dislike Seniors   34

Mate Won't Give Up Closet Space   37

End of Dancing Days   39

Wife Attracted to Other Women   41

Mate Avoids Intimate Conversations   43

When Is It Time To Move On?   45

Leaving Financially Secure Mate   48

3   **Section III - Health Issues Destroying Relationships and Remedies**   51

Sick and Dating   51

ED and A Younger Woman   53

Leaving Mate Because of Diet   55

Garlic Playing Havoc on Relationship   57

Toxic Household Products and
Sex   60

High Blood Pressure, ED and
Sex   63

Testosterone the "Love
Hormone"   66

Manhood Lost to Prostate
Cancer   68

Wife Has "Female Pattern
Baldness"   72

Fighting Off Depression   75

Painful Menstrual Cramps   77

Unbearable Hot Flashes   79

Hysterectomy Ends Sex Life   82

Treat Husband for Yeast
Infection   84

Controlling Outbreaks of Herpes,
Shingles and Urinary Tract
Infections   88

Viagra Side Effects   91

Supplements Raises Sexual
Desires   94

Seeking Sexual Activity Through
Diet   96

Healthier Enough for Sex   98

About the Author   106

PREFACE – A NOTE TO THE READER

This is probably the most difficult book I have ever written. A couple of years ago I became a *"Love Coach"* and started advising others including couples at *DearCathy.com.*

When I first thought about becoming a *"Love Coach,"* I had my doubts about my abilities to motivate people, who were seeking their soulmates.

However, I have known my entire life that I have the ability to bring people together and to let them look at all the possibilities and opportunities, that their lives have to offer.

I would like for everyone to know upfront that this book is not some x-rated book, that will offer you different positions to please your lover in bed.

Instead, it's a book about answering all those too intriguing and important questions, that men and women have about each other as they age.

It's about finding a suitable spouse, partner, mate, significant other or someone that you can enjoy your life with. And mostly, it's about facing the facts in your own life.

I wrote this book because I spent close to 30 years working in a male dominated industry, where my co-workers would ask me all types of questions about their wives or mates. They even called me *"Dr. Ruth."*

Even after a short marriage and being single for many years, I still knew what went on in most relationships and what it took to make them work.

Everyone would like to have a life companion, someone exciting to walk into the sunset with for their remaining years. But if it doesn't happen, it doesn't mean you are not living a worthy life.

Many couples don't want to talk about what it really takes to stay together. Many would rather hide what's obviously broken in their relationships, so that they can go on pretending it doesn't matter.

This results in many years of being unfulfilled and unsatisfied in their relationships. All of it matters, if they ever plan on having a meaningful relationship, or if they ever plan on creating the type of life that they can truly love.

SECTION I – SINGLES OVER 50 LOVE ISSUES

Still Hoping and Searching for Love

Dear Cathy:

I am a 60 year old female and I have been single for a while. I am divorced with no kids and was unhappy in my first marriage, that lasted for 25 years.

I would not say I am desperate, but I would like to have a mate to hold and caress me and make me feel special. Is this even possible anymore for someone that is 60 years old? *Still Hoping and Searching, California*

Dear Still Hoping and Searching:

You are looking for the great American dream. Sometimes, you will have to let go and learn to love yourself first. I would have hoped by age 60, that you would have already learned this.

They say there is someone out there for everyone, so you might have to lower your standards, when trying to find a mate.

However, many men can sense desperation in women and they are trying to avoid these types of women at all costs.

Many men in this country are experiencing Erectile Dysfunction (over 50% at age 40 and over) because of living in toxic environments, eating a toxic diet (GMOs), not exercising or getting enough sleep.

So you need to understand upfront that many men, especially men around your age, lack the desire to take the steps to make any woman feel special.

All this desire, touching and affection, is overrated in many relationships and sometimes for many couples, it will be as good as it get.

Sometimes, relationships can bring headaches and especially heartaches. So you really need to figure out your priorities and take steps to love yourself more.

Happiness is an inside job, so find your happiness within yourself first. You can meet others at http://www.meetup.com, so put all that sexual energy in other things.

Try to get involved with a hobby, business or start traveling. The goal is to fall in love with yourself first. If it is meant to be, it will happen.

Dating a Younger Man

Dear Cathy:

I got a divorce after 30 years. I am now in my early 50s. I moved across country to live with my son, and now I am dating a man 25 years younger than me.

I have not told anyone, including my son and my other children about this man, but he has made me very happy. He does not see the age difference as a problem, but I am sure others will. What do you think? *Dating a Younger Man, Texas*

Dear Dating a Younger Man:

We live in a society that judges women who date younger men, but not men who date younger women, so age is irrelevant when it comes to love.

If dating a younger man has made you happy, then be happy. You are too old to worry about what other people might think of you, including your own children.

Life is meant for you to live, love and be happy. This is your life and at your age, you are setting all the rules, so be happy.

There could be a blessing in disguise here also, for instance, dating a younger man should keep you feeling and looking younger and because of his age, hopefully he doesn't come with too much baggage.

Other women and men, unlike yourself, don't have the courage to do what you are doing. Many remain in loveless marriages, day in and day out, out of a sense of obligation, even though they are not happy.

Not only did you choose to move across the country, but you allowed your heart to be opened again, which is a rarity in these days and times.

Remember, that most people never leave the areas that they grew up in. Therefore, all your efforts to create the life that you truly love, should be applauded.

True Love – But Two Households

Dear Cathy:

I am retired and so is my mate. I have known him for 18 years. He is a neat freak and I am not. After we both retired, he asked me to move in with him.

However, because of his habits, I rather move to his city and maintain my own place instead. Do you think this is a good idea? *Two Households, Missouri*

Dear Two Households:

Many people love each other, but they can't stay under the same roof, especially as they age. Many of these types of relationships have went on for years.

So therefore, it would be a good idea to move to your new city and maintain your own place. Absence truly does make the heart grow fonder, so this type of relationship can be great for the both of you.

Couples need space, especially men, and it might even make you have a stronger relationship, while it prepares the both of you to move in together down the line.

If your mate want you to be in his life, then he will change some of his habits in order to have you there. If he doesn't, then maybe the both of you should think about going separate ways.

But his actions will be key to either growing or ending the relationship. Have regular talks and if you truly see that he is trying to work on things, then again, he might be a keeper.

Mate Won't Destroy Sex Tape

Dear Cathy:

I am in my early 50s and so is a guy that I have been dating. We have been dating each other for a year and have been having a wonderful time.

We both enjoy sex and are in pretty good shape. We like to explore each other, so one night we got really wild and made a sex tape.

He got mad when I found out that he did not destroy it, like I had asked. Should I be worried? *Sex Tape, Maryland*

Dear Sex Tape:

Yes, you should be worried because if that sex tape gets out there, then it will not only embarrass you and your mate, what about your family members?

If your mate want to keep the sex tape as some type of souvenir, then that is just too dangerous to have laying around the house.

What if at his age, there is a medical issue and others come snooping around? What if there is a break up? He can hold that over your head!

He might also have filmed you during other sexual encounters, so at this point I would not trust him at all.

If he is so in love with the sex tape, then there is a chance that something deeper is going on. Is he addicted to porn on the computer or some type of other gadget?

Some men get addicted to porn and it takes over their lives. So look at his desire to hang onto the sex tape, as some type of deeper issue.

In Love With My Friend's Ex

Dear Cathy:

I have been friends with my friend for over 15 years. She got a divorce and is now married to a wonderful man. She never had kids, but now has two stepchildren.

I am secretly dating her ex-husband, who was married to her for 20 years. I wasn't attracted to him when they were together, but now I really love this man.

I don't know what to do about our situation. Do you have any suggestions on how we should handle this? How do I tell my friend that I am in love with her ex-husband or should my new mate tell her, since they are still friends? *Ex-husband Jitters, Boston*

Dear Ex-Husband Jitters:

Falling in love with a friend's ex-husband is a very complicated situation. No one would actually choose to fall in love with a friend's ex-husband.

Since it has happened to you, then you need to deal with it, and you should be the one who breaks this news to her.

One woman's loss is another woman's gain and despite what you think, she might be happy for you. So you need to let her know what has happened.

However, you might be left with the choice of choosing to stay friends, or giving up your new mate. So you need to ask yourself, how important is her friendship.

True love is a rarity and it only comes around once for many people in this lifetime, so I would think about your decision wisely.

Meet with your friend or send her a written letter and explain to her what has happened. Let her know that during the time of her marriage, nothing out of the ordinary or no attractions took place.

She is now married to another man and is probably happy, so again, she might just be happy for you too, especially since she and her ex-husband remained friends after the split.

If that doesn't work, then you might need to avoid her by not hanging out in places, where you know she will be.

But you also need to understand, that true friends don't stand in the way of another friend's happiness.

New Mate Too Clingy

Dear Cathy:

I was married for 19 years. At age 52 I am enjoying the single life. I am about 5 years away from retirement.

I met a woman about 2 months ago, who is 15 years younger than me. She is a beautiful, charming woman and all my family and friends have told me that I lucked out, when I met her.

Everything has been going fine up until now, however, she calls me too much when I am at work. And sometimes, she just shows up where she know I will be.

This is very new for me because I was married for a long time. I have never had a relationship like this before, so how should I handle it? *Clingy Mate, Ohio*

Dear Clingy Mate:

Remember, no two relationships are ever the same and it sounds like this person is really into you. If she calls you too much on your job, then you need to let her know that.

What she is doing is her way of showing you that she cares. Sometimes, women can get too clingy because they just want to make sure that you are still into them. So show her you are still into her by spending time with her.

If you think about her when you are away from her, then just tell her that. This will make her feel even better and reassure her, that you are still there and that things haven't changed.

When you are out with the fellas or at other locations, give her a call or text because women do get nervous, when you are out with the fellas. Just step away from your buddies and send her a text, which will only take a few seconds.

Give her compliments when you are with her.

Women want to know that you notice different things about them, so give her compliments. Most women just want to be appreciated.

If you do all of these things, then she will know you are still into her, and will probably stop being so clingy, and she will trust you more.

Not only will she stop being clingy, but she'll be in a rush to show you just how special you are, if you know what I mean.

In Abusive Relationship

Dear Cathy:

I am 57 and have been divorced for 14 years. My new mate and I both work out all the time. He is in really good shape, so I have a strong attraction for him.

However, it seems that every time I meet a man, he turns out to be abusive. What am I doing wrong that I have to meet these types of men? *Abusive Men, Alabama*

Dear Abusive Men:

The first sign that a relationship will be abusive,

you need to get away from it. It is too many good men out there, that would be willing to treat you like a queen.

So don't allow a man to disrespect you in any way, especially mentally or physically, so look for all the warning signs.

Is he hot-tempered? Does he lose control at the drop of a hat? Does he yell? Does he use profanity around you? Does he experience road rage? Does he try to control everything in the relationship?

These are all warning signs that something more might be going on, and these are the types of relationships you need to back away from. And also look at how he treats other women, especially his mother.

Some men were raised to treat women horribly, so you need to understand that. Some women are so desperate to be in relationships, that they settle for any man interested in them, even though, chances are, these men are up to no good.

Before moving on to another relationship, try to use this time to work on your own self. Find a hobby, start a business or just spend some quiet time everyday meditating or engaging in yoga, which are the best two exercises for your brain.

Some women have a void in their lives, so they try to fill these voids with relationships that are no good for them. Instead, you should fulfill your own needs, something outside of a relationship.

When "Mr. Right" do show up in your life, he will recognize that you are a queen and will treat you like one. He will treat you like someone to be cherished and adored, instead of someone to mentally or physical abuse, but again, you need to work on yourself first.

Mate is the Jealous Type

Dear Cathy:

I am in my early 60s. My new mate is the jealous type, so I haven't told her about my best friend, who I have known for 10 years, who is also a woman.

Even though I have kept them apart so far, eventually, they will have to meet. How should I handle this? *Jealous Type, Illinois*

Dear Jealous Type:

Not telling your new mate about your best friend being a women is a form of dishonestly, so you should come clean as soon as possible.

By not doing this, you are taking trust away from your relationship at the very beginning, so you definitely don't want to do that.

Most women are only jealous of men, who have given them something to be jealous of - have you? Think about your past actions around her.

Many times jealous types can change, especially if they find out your best friend, who is another female, have a serious relationship of her own.

But if she is single and beautiful, then many women, who really care about you, will choose to be jealous of the relationship.

Therefore, you need to make sure that you do not put your friendship over your relationship. Relationships always come before friendships.

You can put your mate at ease when you are away from each other, by sharing your whereabouts with her, especially when she ask you - how your day went.

Many men who are true to their mates, should not really see an issue with keeping their mates informed on their actions and whereabouts, while they were away from each other.

It's called sharing your life together. So you should not find this hard to do, unless you have something to hide.

Dating Outside My Race

Dear Cathy:

I am an African American woman in my 50s. I was single for many years and never had any quality dates. I have now chosen to date outside my race.

I am dating a Caucasian man and my family have stopped talking to me, because of this. This man and I have a lot in common and we love one another.

Should I leave him because of my family or should I follow my heart? *Dating Outside My Race, New York*

Dear Dating Outside My Race:

What families need to understand is that most women want love, affection, sincerity, and to be provided for in most relationships. However, this is easier said than done.

At the end of the night when the lights are turned off, all men feel the same. They are more alike -- than different.

Many black athletes, celebrities, and even others heavily involved in black culture, such as Julian Bond, Maya Angelou, and Alice Walker, have been involved in relationships for years with other nationalities, and no one thought less of them.

Remember, you can't live your life for other people. You can only live your life for your own self, so do what feels right for you.

Love is love and the bottom line is we are only on this earth a short time, and no one should have to walk through this life alone.

So the real goal should be for you to find true happiness in any way, shape or form, which might mean dating outside your race.

Bald Men Make Better Lovers

Dear Cathy:

Is it true that bald men have a higher sex drive and might make better lovers, than men with hair? *Seeking Bald Lover, Michigan*

Dear Seeking Bald Lover:

Yes, it is true, so ladies don't count out bald men. It's every woman's dream, to have a mate with a high sex drive, and women love men with bald heads.

For about 50% of men, hair loss is a reality. Losing your hair at a young age can be pretty depressing, but it also has its benefits.

At first, it can be tragic, depressing, a horrible reminder of immortality, but once a guy realizes it's just a fact of life, and learn to own it, they become even more of a catch, than they ever thought possible.

Having a bald head could mean a higher sex drive because the more testosterone a man has, the thinner his hair. And, high levels of testosterone are linked to higher sex drives in men.

Other benefits include – they are less likely to develop testicular tumors because higher levels of testosterone offer some protection; Their physical assets like dimples, long eye lashes and pearly whites pops out; They might be better at sports because many men who are good at sports are bald; They are low maintenance, which many women like; They save big bucks on hair products and they master how to wear a hat because no one can wear a hat like a bald guy.

Again, many women love men with bald heads, so guys need to get over it and enjoy the many benefits of being bald.

Getting Breast Implants for Mate

Dear Cathy:

I recently moved to California and have been dating a beautiful man for the past year. I have always had a flat chest and I absolutely don't like it.

My new mate, who is 55, I am 50, tells me all the time that I have a knock out body, but it would be even better if I had more upfront.

I basically agree with him and is thinking about getting breast implants. I know the operation will boost my self-esteem and give me even more confidence. What do you think? *Breast Implants, California*

Dear Breast Implants:

Basically, you need to do what is best for you, but I would definitely conduct more research before going under the knife.

Sometimes, there are issues when you are put to sleep during any type of surgery, such as many times doctors leave scissors, sponges and other equipment in patients, when they operate. And many patients just don't wake up!

Also many breast implants can be toxic and end up leaking through the skin, maybe not right away, but down the line, so make sure you conduct extensive research and learn more about the type of implants, you will be receiving.

Before your surgery, talk to other women who have had the type of implants that you will be receiving, to see if they have had any issues with them. Talk to as many women as possible.

There are many ways to boost your self-esteem and confidence that don't involve surgery. Basically, you need to conduct research on your brain and how it works to send positive signals throughout your body.

You need to eat good brain foods and take brain supplements because your foods affects every area of your life -- from your mood, to your behavior, happiness and your entire quality of life.

Many men would not want you to do this, especially at such a late stage in your life. So if you are doing this to please a man, again rethink your decision. However, remember in the end, only you can make this important decision.

21

SECTION II – COUPLES OVER 50 LOVE ISSUES

Sick of Being Sexless in Seattle

Dear Cathy:

My husband and I are in our early 50s and we have not had sex in over 2 years. We have been married for 21 years and have always had a strong sex drive.

I crave the warmth of intimacy. Even though I try to initiate sex, he is often turned off. Is there anything that we can do, besides seeing a family or sex therapist? *Sexless in Seattle*

Dear Sexless:

If he is turned off and doesn't have any desire to be with you, then maybe he needs to see a doctor first, to make sure he doesn't have a form of Erectile Dysfunction (ED) or some type of other health issue.

Men don't like going to doctors for regular checkups, but he should make sure all his important numbers stay in range, such as blood pressure, blood glucose, cholesterol, trigylcerides, etc.

What most people, especially couples, don't understand is that their diets are key to having a strong sex life.

You are indeed what you eat and foods can affect your mood, behavior, happiness and entire quality of life.

If you and your family are eating processed foods containing Genetically Modified Organisms (GMOs), then your husband will have a low libido or low sex drive.

Every community has a natural and holistic community. Health and wholefood stores will offer FREE and low-cost health and wellness lectures, seminars, and workshops.

They will also know where families can gain access to local organic farmers, who can provide classes and teach everyone what to grow and when to grow it.

The key is education. Once he starts eating a holistic and natural diet, engage in a regular exercise program and get plenty of sleep, then everything should go back to normal.

Also, the both of you should look at cleaning up your inside environment, by using only natural products on your body and to clean with.

Wife Seeks More Intimacy

Dear Cathy:

I am 54 and my husband is 56. Our children are all grown and live away from home. We don't have any grandkids yet either.

My husband and I have not had sex in over a year. Since he works shift work at night from 12:00 midnight to 8:00 a.m., 6 days a week, our relationship could be classified as roommates, rather than husband and wife.

I am home from my job by 4:00 p.m. everyday, but that's when he is catching up on his sleep for his midnight shift. What can we do to get the intimacy back? *Intimacy Seeker, Oregon*

Dear Intimacy Seeker:

I know your husband works shifts work, but the goal is to try to still get some alone time together to be intimate, because your marriage is also important.

One solution I see up front is to have your husband get on another shift, but if this is not possible, then you need to work around his schedule.

If he works shift work, then he needs to sleep during the day, while you are at work. He could still take a nap or get more sleep before his midnight shift starts.

There are many things you can do with your spouse to bond once you get off work. You could work out together outside or at the gym, go to movies, dinner or just long walks.

On his one day off, especially plan some alone time together. You have to plan this just like a date. So sit down and talk with your husband about what you really need.

Remember, *"Men Are from Mars, Women Are from Venus,"* which is a book that all women and men should read, so they can better understand each other.

Most men have no idea what a woman really need. Just let him know that your intimate relationship is just as important as his job, so communication will be key to getting your point across.

Couple Need to Shop Online

Dear Cathy:

My husband is 51 years old and I am 50. We still have a great sex life and like trying new things. However, he wants me to visit an adult sex store.

The problem is, I know other shop owners next to the store, so I am too embarrassed to go into this store. I told him I would only go in the store if I wore a disguise. What should I do?
Embarrassed, Arizona

Dear Embarrassed:

Don't stress about it! Wearing sunglasses or some sort of disguise will only draw more attention to you.

Think of it this way, if you run into someone you know, then you need to realize they are there for the same purpose, so who are they to judge.

Once you've been able to get over the initial anxiety of going in the store, you'll be fine. I am certain you are not the first person that has felt this way.

However, judging by the age of both of you, you both must be old school and not *'tech saavy'* because today, you can buy everything online.

So, instead of being paranoid about being seen in neighborhood sex shops, whatever your husband and you are looking for, you will be able to look for it and just purchase it online.

Go to Google.com and put in the words "online sex store" or "online adult sex store" and you will have the world at your fingertips. If you don't like shopping online, then look for other sex stores in other areas in your city.

Over 50% of men have some form of Erectile Dysfunction (ED) or is impotent by age 40, so for your husband and you to still want to play sex games, both of you should be commended and congratulated.

Husband Left Alone on New Years

Dear Cathy:

I have been married for 5 years and my husband and I are both in our early 50s. My husband don't really acknowledge holidays and said he did not really want to go out on

New Year's eve, so I went out with some ladies from my job.

He is a homebody and I am just the opposite, who crave being around other people. Was it wrong for me to go out without him?

This was the first time that I left him alone on a holiday, and even though he hasn't said anything, I think it made him upset that I chose to do this? *Partying With Friends, Oklahoma*

Dear Partying With Friends:

Many people would say you were wrong to leave your husband at home during such a big and special day, but if he insisted that you bring in the New Year without him, then I don't see a problem with it.

Some men are just not into holidays. They never have been and probably never will be. The fact that he initially told you it was okay, should have took away your doubts about it.

However, if he has treated you differently since you made that decision, might show that he really did not believe you would make that decision, even though he left it strictly up to you.

Anyway, now it's time to mend fences. You need to sit down and reassure him that even though you were out partying with your friends, that he was the only person on your mind.

Do something special for him like bring him flowers or a card. Men try to let on like they don't like these things, but deep inside, some men enjoy this, just as much as some women.

Do something romantic also like plan a trip out of town, or prepare a special dinner for the two of you to celebrate your love. Like women, men just need extra attention and reassurance, that you truly love them.

Husband Can't Say He Loves Wife

Dear Cathy:

I am a widow and I have been married for two years. My husband and I have a pretty good relationship, however, he can't say the words *"I Love You."*

We both are in our middle 50s and my former husband use to tell me all the time, that he loved me. However, my new husband can't say the words.

He says he has a hard time saying it and it is just words, and that I should know he loves me, without him needing to verbalize it.

While I do know he loves me, I still feel the need to hear it, and it hurts that he can't say it, even when it means so much to me.

Am I making a big deal out of nothing, or do I have the right to want my husband to say the words? *Need to Hear It, Georgia*

Dear Need To Hear It:

The situation you mention is unfortunately all too common. It is true that certain people have a hard time communicating in general.

This is especially true when it comes to stating words of love. However, many women especially, need to hear the words.

It is a great start that you know your husband loves you, but as you state, it is a different thing altogether to hear the words spoken.

Some men will show you, instead of saying the words. Clearly, it is better to be shown love and witness acts of love, rather than being told words of love that are empty.

However, that still does not take away the need or desire to hear the words. The concept of needing to hear words of love is a legitimate and real need. And one that needs to be met, if at all possible.

It is considerably more difficult for a man to state words of love, than it is for a woman. This doesn't mean that all men have difficulty verbalizing their feelings, and for all women it is easy.

The lack of verbal reassurance of his love is something that the two of you should discuss, as he needs to be aware of how difficult it is for you, when he won't say *"I Love You."*

On the other hand, you should be sensitive to the fact that it is difficult for him to verbally express himself. It is unfair to deny him words of love, simply because he may not think to say them on his own.

Hopefully, by you saying them to him, it will remind and encourage him to share such words in return.

Married to a Homebody

Dear Cathy:

My husband and I are both retired at age 62. He doesn't have a lot of friends. He has spent a lot of money on our home, making it comfortable for the both of us.

The problem is, now that he has fixed up our home, I can't get him out of the house to save my life. He use to at least take me out to dinner, a movie, a drive and a walk, but now I can't get him out of the house.

He keeps busy by doing chores around the house, working in the yard or fixing something up at home during the day.

After that, he eats dinner and props himself up in front of the TV, until the wee hours of the night. How can I get him to look at me again, and treat me like I should be treated? *Sick of Being With A Homebody, Alabama*

Dear Sick of Being With a Homebody:

When couples retire, they think their life will be one way, but it may turn out to be another way, so don't get frustrated.

Sometimes, especially when men ages, they get set in their ways and want to do things only the way they want to do them, and when they want to do them.

So trying to get him unstuck from these bad habits, will probably be extremely hard. By making your home comfortable for the both of you, he is saying that his home is his castle.

You need to understand that many people are homebodies. Being a homebody means that they get more joy out of being at home, and remember many people do shy away from crowds.

However, even though he has made your home comfortable for the both of you, relationships just don't involve staying at home all the time, so tell him how you feel.

Just because he is a homebody, doesn't mean you also need to be a homebody. There are plenty of things you can do to bring more joy and happiness into your life.

If he is still unresponsive to your needs, get female friends, take up activities and hobbies without him. Get a traveling companion and do things outside of your home -- without him.

You can start by going to meetup.com for a wide variety of choices, or you can form your own meetup.com group around activities you enjoy.

When he sees that you have other activities taking you away from home, it might interest him again to look at other activities, especially activities that can involve the both of you, so don't give up. Just remember, absence does make the heart grow fonder.

Senior Couple Dislike Seniors

Dear Cathy:

My husband and I are in our early 70s. We never had any children. We led a very positive life, and we both enjoy traveling to different places.

Even though we are retired, we only have a small retirement to fall back on. At our age we are always looking to save money, so we can enjoy traveling and other things.

We are thinking about selling our home and downsizing into an apartment or condo. The apartments that we are looking at renting is

$600 a month, but at our ages, we could pay $450 to live in a senior community.

Are we shallow for not wanting to live around other seniors, even though we could save more money for traveling and other things?

My husband and I are still active. But today it seems that many seniors have given up on life. Therefore, we rather not deal with the negativity that we feel living in a senior community could bring.

Does this makes sense and are we shallow for thinking like this? *Shallow About Seniors, Tennessee*

Dear Shallow About Seniors:

No, you are not shallow for not wanting to live around other seniors. This is your life and no one can make you do something you don't want to do, especially at your age.

Many seniors and others don't like shopping at stores on senior day, because it will be full of seniors, who often move slowly.

So many seniors, even seniors themselves, don't want to live or be around other seniors.

Again this is strictly your choice.

I believe many seniors think that if they live in senior communities, they will end up assisting seniors bring groceries in, or with other chores.

And many seniors think living around other seniors, especially sick seniors, will remind them of how they will be one day.

As you get older, eventually your body will break down and give out. But what you need to remember is that "Getting old does not make you sick, but getting sick makes you old."

So saving as much money as you can on your rent, to help you buy good food or engage in regular physical activities, will help keep you healthier, including having an active sex life.

Also, many seniors are victims of crime today, so being safe along with eating good food, should be at the front of your list, when you make this decision.

If your new apartment or condo will provide more protection for you, compared to the senior community, then by all means move there, have fun and live a great life.

Mate Won't Give Up Closet Space

Dear Cathy:

I recently moved in a home with a man that I truly love, and have dated for 10 years. We are both retired, so we finally decided to move in together -- in his home.

However, he refused to move most of his items out of his closet to give me room. He has lived alone for a while, and like doing things his way.

He said since I had so many things, I needed to put my things in the extra bedroom, so that I would have the closet space that I needed.

But I feel like he should have been more supportive of me moving in, and allowed me more space in his closet, since it is the biggest closet.

I am having second thoughts about my decision to move in with him. Did I make a mistake by moving in with him? *Move-In Mistake, Florida*

Dear Move-In Mistake:

No, not really, however, not compromising in

the bedroom, might lead to problems down the road, so most men need to understand that.

A woman would like to feel like she belongs in a home, especially when she is invited to move in. If she does not have a say-so about every area of the house, it might cause problems down the line.

On the other hand, placing all your items in the other closet and bedroom, will give you the *'she-cave'* that you probably need, when you just want to relax.

Many men have space issues, so it's always a good idea to have your own space or area in your home, where you can go and relax, when you want to be alone.

Remember as men (and women) ages, they will become too set in their ways, so it will be hard for him to give up his space for you, or make other changes in other areas of his life.

I would not make a big deal out of the living arrangements. See how he treats you, that's the most important thing. If he goes out of his way in other areas to make you feel welcome, then again, I would not make a big deal out of it.

You both are under the same roof, which should give both of you more cozier and fun times with each other. That's all that really matters.

End of Dancing Days

Dear Cathy:

I grew up dancing all the time when I was younger, so it has always been a part of my life. I am in my early 50's and was seeking a mate, who also like to dance, just like my ex-husband, who has passed on.

Dancing has always been an expression of love for me, and I don't want to stop dancing, however, I recently married a man that doesn't enjoy dancing at all.

Since my new mate doesn't enjoy dancing, I guess this is the end of my dancing days. Is there anything that I can do about my mate lack of desire to dance? *End of Dancing Days, New Jersey*

Dear End of Dancing Days:

I agree that dancing is a great expression of love, and no one should have to give it up just because they are now with someone, who doesn't like to dance.

It is definitely not the end of your dancing days. There is a lot you can do to continue dancing. Most communities have different dance groups that meets at meetup.com groups, dance halls or other locations in the city, so ask around and use google.com to find them.

Many have partners to match you with, just to dance. Your mate might even be opened to coming out to the groups and engaging in dancing also, especially if he hears that you will be matched with other male dancers, so ask him. Let him know how important this is to you.

Movement is important, especially as you age, and dancing is a great exercise for you and your spouse, so use every opportunity you can to keep moving.

Also try engaging in regular Zumba, which is just like dancing. You can buy the videos at Zumba.com or even cheaper at Amazon.com, and look for a class at local gyms, or in your neighborhood.

Dancing can also be freeing, so again, I would not give it up just because you ended up with a mate, that doesn't enjoy dancing.

Most couples don't always enjoy the same things, but it doesn't mean they are not meant to be together in this lifetime or that they are not soulmates.

The goal is to keep aging gracefully, and take your love for dancing into your golden years.

Wife Attracted To Other Women

Dear Cathy:

After 25 years of marriage, my wife told me she is attracted to other women. She said she has only acted on this a few times before. But at this point, I can't really trust anything that she says to me.

Every day I wonder where our relationship stands. One day she says she wants to work it out, and the next she says we should get a divorce.

I don't know if I should end our relationship, or wait to see where it goes. I am running out of patience, so what do you think? *Wife Attracted to Women, Connecticut*

Dear Wife Attracted to Women:

Marriages today are extremely hard to deal with. You think you will spend the rest of your life with someone, then something tragic like this happens.

Being attracted to another man or woman is not a crime, but once a spouse acts on those attractions, then it's time for one or both of you to take action.

I would handle your wife's attraction to other women, the same as if she was attracted to other men. I know it can be a shocking and painful situation, that have left a lot of confusion on your part, but being unfaithful is being unfaithful.

If both of you are ever going to survive what is happening, then you will have to take action and move on. The sooner the better, so the both of you can carve out some type of life either together, or away from each other.

Counseling of course is a good first option, but not just counseling to keep you together, you might also want to look at counseling to help you go your separate ways.

Also read the book *"The Other Side of the Closet,"* by Amity Pierce Buxton, Ph.D., and check out this support group entitled the *"Straight Spouse Network"* (StraightSpouse.org), which offers emotional support after a wife or a husband comes out as yours did.

Mate Avoids Intimate Conversations

Dear Cathy:

I got with my mate much later on in my life. I am 50 and my mate is 70 years old. All he wants to do is fall asleep in front of the TV every night, while watching the news.

On the other hand, I want to engage in stimulating and intimate conversations, and feel close to him. I am thinking about leaving him for greener pastures. What do you think? *Greener Pastures, Idaho*

Dear Greener Pastures:

Before you head for the door, your mate needs to go to the doctor to see if there is anything that might be zapping his energy.

Many men are vibrant, even in their 60s, 70s,

80s or 90s, so he could have some type of health issue that he needs to address.

Then you need to look at his diet. However, trying to change the diet of an older person, especially a man, is like pulling teeth, and no one really wants to do that.

Men at his age are too set in their ways. They are not going to do something else or live another way, just to please another person. And this is why many men have chosen to stay single because of this.

I suggest you have a serious talk with him about how you feel, and you might need to figure out, that it is as good as it is going to get.

The age difference might not have been an issue at first, but you need to understand because of his age, there are certain things you will have to give up.

Even though many men go into their 60s, 70s, 80s and even 90s with a high sex drive, once they lose their libido and are not good conversationalist, then it might be time to move on, because it will then be as good as you are going to get.

You have a right to want more, especially at your age. Sure when the relationship started, the both of you were all bright-eyed and bushy-tailed, but again because of his age, everything is different now.

Now like most women your age, you need to decide if this is what you bargained for, or are you seriously ready to move on.

Everyone would like to have a life companion, someone exciting with whom to walk into the sunset with for their remaining years, but if it doesn't happen, it doesn't mean you are not living a worthy life. Only you can decide if you are truly ready to move on.

When Is It Time to Move On?

Dear Cathy:

I have been married for 24 years. My husband and I are both in our early 50s. My husband is always negative. He has no friends of his own and he constantly sits around the house and complain, complain, complain.

We chose not to have kids and I am thinking about leaving him, however, my finances tells me I can't go anywhere. What do you suggest?

Need To Leave Marriage, Florida

Dear Need To Leave Marriage:

Many people are just negative - the naysayers, the doom and gloom people, and no matter what you do or say, they will not change.

Do whatever you have to, to make it work, but if you are at the end of your rope, then it's definitely time to move on.

Make a list of the pros and cons of your marriage, tally them up and weigh the cons against how you feel living the life, you are living now.

Many men need to understand the phrase *"Happy Wife, Happy Life,"* but many never got the memo. In other words, if men don't keep their wives happy, then they are in for a rude awakening.

Many women have stated the same facts that you are stating today, but many stay while many, many others leave.

Despite being in unhappy relationships, many women stay because they are too afraid to live alone, or they don't see anything better on the horizon.

But why waste the most valuable years of your life on someone who could give two cents about how you feel and what you really need.

Not being financially secure should not be a reason to stay in a worthless marriage. It all depends on if you truly want to explore other options and take action in your life.

Try reaching out to family members or friends to see if you can move in while you become more financially secure, with another job or your own business.

That option has got to be better than what you are putting up with at this time. A licensed counselor may be able to steer you in the right direction.

This could include working with a marriage counselor to hang onto the marriage, or consulting a lawyer and getting a divorce.

There is probably a man out there that will love you, and would love to make you happy. But you will never know this, if you continue to stay in a loveless, negative, worthless marriage. So the ball is in your court.

Leaving Financially Secure Mate

Dear Cathy:

At 55, I am being wooed by 2 different suitors, who live in other states. One I think I could be happier with, even though I have been living with my current mate for over a year.

My current mate and I have a long history together, an on-again, off-again relationship for the past 20 years.

Even though I have not been unfaithful to him, six months ago he stopped showing any affections toward me. He stopped kissing me or giving me hugs.

I have tried to talk to him about issues he might be having, but he abruptly tells me he doesn't want to talk about anything.

I am the type of person who likes intimacy in a relationship. So I am torn between leaving him because of his lack of desire for affection for me, even though he is financially secure.

So is leaving my financially secure mate a real option for me? What should I do? *Financially*

Secure Mate, San Diego

Dear Financially Secure Mate:

Six months is a very long time, but before bolting for the door, first talk to your mate and ask him if you both can see a family counselor, or even a sex therapist.

Many men don't like going to doctors and they keep secrets about their health. So try to talk to him to see if there is anything going on.

If he is not opened to the idea of working with counselors and therapists, then maybe it's time to try something new.

However, instead of jumping from relationship to relationship, maybe you need to spend some time alone to work on your own self.

Many men (and women) don't know that they are making their mates unhappy, and sometimes you might even need to put it in a letter.

The goal, however, is to get your point across to him, so that you can explore other options. Remember, *"Men Are from Mars, Women Are from Venus,"* which is a book that all couples should read.

Life is short and despite being with someone who is financially secure, money don't make anyone happy, and it certainly can't buy happiness.

Just remember, however, that the pastures are not always greener on the other side. You might need to work on loving your own self, before making a leap to leave your mate, or before jumping into another relationship.

You have a long history with your mate, so ask yourself if you are actually being true to yourself, and trying to work things out, or is your mate totally unresponsive to your needs.

But still, I would not stay with anyone that is totally ignoring your needs. Again, life is too short and there are plenty of fish in the sea.

SECTION III – HEALTH ISSUES DESTROYING RELATIONSHIPS AND REMEDIES

Sick and Dating

Dear Cathy:

I have been diagnosed with liver disease. At this point I have very few friends and my skin looks jaundiced. So should I still try to date? *Sick and Dating, Ohio*

Dear Sick and Dating:

At this point the only thing that should be on your mind is your illness, and what you can do to get well again.

There will be plenty of time to date once you take a hold of your health, but for now you need to look at what is happening to your body.

The liver is one of the most important organs in your body. It's the largest detoxification organ in your body.

What's unfortunate is that most people's livers are only operating at 30%, so eventually many people will be diagnosed with liver disease and other preventable diseases.

If people don't do what they can to strengthen their liver and other organs, then they won't have a fighting chance, because organ failure is the number one reason that most people don't make it.

Despite what a doctor might tell you, the body has the enormous ability to heal itself. Therefore, I would seek out holistic and natural communities, which are located in every city, and work with these healers and experts, to get your health back on track.

Remember that your foods are your medicine, so don't allow doctors to put you on all these medications, which will do nothing but cause your body to deteriorate even faster.

Once you start eating healing foods, especially foods that supports your liver and other organs, and foods for your blood type, you will have a fighting chance to survive your ordeal.

The people that you are trying to meet while dating will not understand your predicament, so why try to explain it to them.

Why put your energy there, when all your energy should be used to focus on getting well again, and living a long, vibrant life.

Once you figure out what you need to do to move forward and take control of your own health, there will be plenty of time for dating.

ED and A Younger Woman

Dear Cathy:

I am 60 years old but in love with a 30 year old woman. She has 4 kids, ages 3, 5, 7 and 9. I am in love with all of them. We are planning on getting married soon, and I want to provide for all of them, if something happens to me.

The problem is, I have an Erectile Dysfunction (ED) problem, however, she claims she doesn't care about that. I was young once and somehow I just don't believe her. What should I do to protect myself? Could she just be a gold-digger? *Gold-digger, Arkansas*

Dear Gold-digger:

Talking about baggage, many older men don't want to get with younger women, with such a young family, unless they are seeking the family they never had, so I admire you for this.

Certainly, she can be a gold-digger, which is a woman who associates with a man chiefly for material gain. However, many younger women do prefer older men because of their maturity.

Maybe she doesn't care about the sex because at this point, with such a young family, she is probably just trying to make sure her kids have what they need.

Mothers always put their kids first. However, in the future, it might become a problem. So protect yourself by providing a prenuptial agreement.

Also discuss with a lawyer, who specializes in wills and trusts, about the best way to leave money or assets in a trust for the kids after they reach a certain age, so the money can't be dispersed prematurely.

Meanwhile, go ahead and get with this woman and have fun. There are many benefits to being with a younger partner, who can also help take care of you as you transition into your golden years.

She might also be in a position to help you

figure out what is causing your ED, which can be caused by certain foods, medications, low testosterone, and other things, so again take the risk.

Leaving Mate Because of Diet

Dear Cathy:

I moved in with my mate that I have known for 12 years in another state, after we both retired. I never wanted to end up with a mate that ate really bad foods.

My mate should be known as the *'Poster Boy'* for eating bad foods. I am a healthy and conscious eater and he is not. So we agreed to buy and fix our own meals.

However, sometimes, at least once or twice a week, he brings enough food home for the both of us, so he tempts me to eat the bad foods.

On several occasions, I have found myself eating these bad foods, which makes me feel sick and horrible later on.

Plus the foods makes me feel weak, sluggish and run-down and this is probably another reason, why he constantly complains about being tired.

I am so unhappy with his behavior, but he won't stop this, so I am thinking about moving out. What should I do? *Bad Foods, Virginia*

Dear Bad Foods:

This is a major issue for many couples, who get together later on in life. Many couples have even chosen to get two refrigerators because of this.

One thing for sure is you will not be able to change a man in his 50s or 60s because by these ages, they are just too set in their ways. But if you truly love him, try to work something out.

Yes, bad foods will make you feel weak, sluggish and run-down, but many people have not been able to make this connection yet.

This is where will-power and self-discipline will play a vital role in your life. Make sure he understands beyond a shadow of a doubt, how you feel about the foods that he eats, and tell him that you feel he is tempting you to eat the bad foods also.

Maybe he thinks he is taking care of you, or providing for you by buying enough foods for the both of you. But when he sees that you are not eating the foods and that the foods are going to waste, then he should get the message.

Garlic Playing Havoc on Relationship

Dear Cathy:

I am really into my health. I watched my father and mother both die horrifying deaths from being sick for a long time.

Therefore, I conducted my own research and know that garlic is extremely good for anyone trying to bring their health under control.

I have been single for a while, but finally met a nice guy in his 50s. The problem is, I eat garlic 3 times a day and no matter what type of breath mints I take, it still can't cover the taste of the garlic.

My mate said he hates kissing me. I am torn between staying single and being healthy versus stopping eating garlic. What should I do? *Garlic Breath, North Carolina*

Dear Garlic Breath:

First of all, I want to thank you for being proactive in regards to your health, but pay attention to what I am about to say to you.

Relationships are hard and if you have a keeper, then you need to do what you can to make it work. Don't let something like eating garlic stand in your way.

The best way to get rid of garlic breath is to stop eating it. This is the only way to completely eliminate garlic breath.

Garlic and other members of the allium plant family, including onions, shallots, and leeks, produce cysteine sulfoxide and this gives them their distinct odor and taste.

Even if you neutralize the garlic breath compounds in the mouth, it will still be exhaled from your lungs, still making your breath smell like garlic. So it is difficult for you to know if you have garlic breath, or how bad it really is.

Remedies you can do include to eat parsley, because a lot of times recipes that use garlic, also use parsley as well, and parsley is effective in neutralizing the odors of garlic. You can try chewing on parsley after eating garlic.

You can also try eating lemons. Try sucking on a lemon wedge after eating garlic. A lemon is very effective in neutralizing the garlic odor and it also has anti-bacterial properties, that will kill bacteria. Also washing your hands with lemon juice helps to remove the odor from your hands.

Another remedy includes drinking tea. Drink tea while or after eating garlic. Tea, especially green and peppermint, contain polyphenols that reduce the volatile sulfur compounds, that the garlic produces.

You also need to look at chewing gum, especially sugar-free-gum. This will help to mask the odor of the garlic, and will help dislodge garlic and food particles, that might be stuck on or between your teeth.

If removing garlic from your diet is not an option, you can cut back on the garlic. You can eat it once a day or every other day, but you do not need to eat garlic 3 times a day for it to be effective.

This way it will still be in your system to help you boost your immune system, and for other health benefits.

Don't forget, however, the biggest solution to this problem is to just buy odorless garlic supplements from health or wholefood stores, which your mate will not notice.

Toxic Household Products and Sex

Dear Cathy:

I am 61 and very health conscious. I spent most of my life single and raising my children after my husband passed away, very early on in our marriage.

For years I have carried on an on-again, off-again long-distance relationship. We both truly love each other, but traveling back and forth got to be really expensive.

So after we both retired, I decided to travel to his state and move in with him. We both have had health issues in the past.

The only problem is now that I am totally natural from head to toe, and eat only a natural and organic diet, he still won't allow me to remove toxic cleaning products from our home.

We both have agreed to prepare our own meals, since he still insists on eating processed foods. But how can I get him to understand the dangers of using these toxic cleaning and body products in our home and why removing them will be key to living healthier lives, especially a healthier and proactive sex life? *Frustrated Mate on the West Coast*

Dear Frustrated Mate:

If your mate desire you to stay there in his home, then he needs to conform to some of your demands. However, instead of pushing him, you need to first try to educate him on why these toxic products can be harmful, especially to your sex life.

Breathing in toxic products in your home, especially when you clean and use them on your skin, will zap your energy and keep you from being able to reach your full potential.

The liver, the organ in charge of *energy* (also emotions and obesity), will not be able to give you the energy you will need, to have a long and proactive sex life, which every couple should desire.

Let him know that most people's livers are already only operating at 30%, so using natural products will be key to having tons of energy and vitality as you age.

Try to educate him by bringing home reading material that he can read, educational videos that both of you can watch together, and join holistic and natural communities, which are located in every city.

If that doesn't work and you truly want to be with your mate, then it's a good idea to have separate facilities at your home.

Many couples are happy sleeping in different bedrooms, especially since a lot of men snore; they have their own bathrooms because many women need their own space; they have separate closets because many women have more clothes than men; they have separate refrigerators because many times one partner might not like looking at all the unhealthy foods; and many even use their own natural dish and washing detergents, natural cleaning solutions, including natural products they put on their skin.

This is a great way to avoid some of these toxic body and cleaning products, so do whatever works. Since most women are in charge of buying groceries, body products and cleaning supplies for the home, hopefully he will eventually come around, so the both of you can take care of each other as you age gracefully.

High Blood Pressure, ED and Sex

Dear Cathy:

When my husband and I first got married, 20 years ago, and had two kids, we had an active sex life. But things have changed over the past few years.

We are both in our late 50s and my husband hasn't touched me in over a year, especially after going on medications for high blood pressure.

He was also told by the family doctor that he has Erectile Dysfunction (ED), but he refuses to take the medication for that.

Can you explain further what exactly is Erectile Dysfunction (ED) and is this something that can be corrected naturally? *Lack of Knowledge on ED, Pittsburgh*

Dear Lack Knowledge on ED:

Both high blood pressure and Erectile Dysfunction (ED) can be corrected through his diet, unless the ED was caused by some type of prostate surgery, which can cause shrinkage in most men. Like most diseases, high blood pressure and ED are *"food-related"* diseases.

Most men have ED today because of their toxic diets. Other reasons men get ED include men with diabetes develop ED 10 to 15 years earlier, so stop eating any sweets or white processed foods, which turns into sugar in your body and causes diabetes. Read my book *"Diabetes 101: 3rd Largest Killer"* at http://www.AngelsPress.com to find out more.

Other reasons for ED include medications for diabetes, high blood pressure, high cholesterol, antidepressants, diuretics, antihistamines, sedatives, and steroids causes ED.

Also alcohol, drugs and nicotine use causes ED. So does a zinc deficiency, heated car seats, laptops, and low testosterone.

The trick is to get off the high blood pressure medication before the doctor recommend more medications.

Once many people go on high blood pressure medications, most people, especially seniors, end up on 3 to 4 (or more) different medications, just for high blood pressure.

Over 50% of men over age 40 have some form of Erectile Dysfunction (ED) or impotence because most families today are eating toxic Genetically Modified (GM) foods (processed foods).

These foods causes impotence and sterility in men and infertility in women and they also have ED because of living in toxic environments inside of their homes.

Citrus fruit is good for sperm. Helpful herbs includes saw palmetto and Siberian ginseng. Don't take ginseng with high blood pressure and some blood types should not take ginseng, so read the book *"Eat Right 4 Your Type."*

The pharmaceutical industry is big business, so it will not be in your doctor's interest to help your husband get off these medications, so he will have to do this on his own.

Once your family gain access to safe and

natural foods and start eating foods in as natural forms as possible, while he engage in a regular exercise program and get plenty of rest, he will be able to lower his blood pressure and get his sex life back on track.

Testosterone the "Love Hormone"

Dear Cathy:

I have a hard time getting my husband to have regular checkups at the doctor's office. He is only 53 with a very low sex drive and I am thinking it might be his testosterone.

At what age should my husband have his testosterone level checked and why is testosterone considered to be the *"Love Hormone"*? *Low Sex Drive, Philadelphia*

Dear Low Sex Drive:

Years ago, the medical industry told all men to have their testosterone level checked at age 50, but because of toxic GMO foods and toxic cleaning and body products, they are telling all men today to get checked at age 35, or even earlier.

They call Testosterone, *Low T,* and it is known

as the *"Love Hormone."* Testosterone is a hormone that is produced by the human body and is mainly produced in the testicles in men.

It stimulates sperm production and a man's sex drive, and also helps build muscle and bone mass. During puberty, testosterone helps build a man's muscles, deepens his voice, and boosts the size of his penis and testes.

In adulthood, it keeps a man's muscles and bones strong, and maintains his interest in sex. After age 30, most men begin to experience a gradual decline in testosterone.

Some of the symptoms include low sex drive; low semen volume, which can cause infertility; hair loss; fatigue and lack of energy; loss of muscle mass; increase in body fat; decrease in bone mass and mood changes.

Testosterone influences many physical processes in the body. It can also influence mood and mental capacity, including depression, irritability, or a lack of focus.

Treatments include testosterone injections; A daily gel or patch; and they can implant pellets in a man's rear, which can release testosterone over the course of 3 to 4 months.

There are also side effects, so tell your husband to use a natural supplement from a health or wholefood store instead.

Testosterone treatments can raise a man's red blood cell count, as well as enlarge his breasts, and accelerate prostate growth.

Therefore, treatments are not advised for men with or at risk for prostate cancer. Again, if I was him, I would only seek out natural supplements from health or wholefood stores.

Manhood Lost To Prostate Cancer

Dear Cathy:

Our children are all grown up and now we are grandparents, who still enjoy an active sex life. However, I am starting to have trouble with my prostate.

My father and brother both had prostate cancer. They are doing fine after surgery, but my brother said he no longer enjoys sex.

What do I need to know about prostate cancer? Is it hereditary and can it also take my manhood? *Family History of Prostate Cancer, Sacramento*

Dear Family History of Prostate Cancer:

If you end up with Prostate Cancer, the doctor will do one or all 3 of these things – 1) operate, 2) give you radiation, or 3) chemotherapy.

If he operates, you will be left with half the shrinkage, so you will lose your manhood. This is really embarrassing for most men. So your only choice if you ever plan on penetrating a woman again, will be to get a penal implant.

All men should get their prostate checked by age 40, earlier if they have family history. Prostate cancer is the second most common cancer in American men.

African American men have the highest rate of prostate cancer in the world. The risk for prostate cancer increases with age.

Prostate cancer usually occurs in older men and most often appears after age 50, but can appear at an earlier age, especially today because of the toxic world that we live in.

Men, even in their early 40s, are dying of prostate cancer. Diets are certainly a factor. Family history also plays a role because most families were raised eating the same diets.

If a man's father or brother has cancer of the prostate, his risk is two to three times greater than average, however, most diseases are not hereditary, but instead *"food-related."*

Men who eat large amounts of animal fat, particularly fats from red meat, may face a greater risk of prostate cancer, than men who eat less animal fat.

Prostate cancer forms in tissues of the prostate (a gland in the male reproductive system). The prostate produces semen, the fluid that carries sperm. The prostate gland is found below the bladder and in front of the rectum.

Normally, the prostate is about the size of a walnut. As a man gets older, the prostate often becomes enlarged. More than one-half of American men over the age of 60, have some enlargement of the prostate. This is not usually caused by cancer, but could possibly cause other problems.

Often, there are no symptoms in the early stages of prostate cancer. If symptoms do occur, they can vary, depending on the size and exact location of the lump, or the growth in the prostate.

Since the prostate surrounds the urethra, the tube that carries urine and semen, any change in the prostate can cause problems with urination and ejaculation.

However, similar symptoms can be caused by a number of things, including an infection or a non-cancerous condition called Benign Prostatic Hyperplasia (BPH).

If a man has problems with a weak or interrupted flow or pain while urinating, painful ejaculation, blood in the urine or semen, or a nagging pain in the back, hips or pelvis, he should see a health care provider or an urologist to find out what's going on.

The only way to detect prostate cancer is by taking a PSA test or getting a rectal exam. Saw palmetto, green tea and zinc supplements from health or wholefood stores aids in preventing prostate cancer.

Cancer is the 2nd largest killer in the U.S. Just remember that cancer is an immune system, food and environmental disease.

Once you strengthen your immune system, clean up your diet and your inside environment, you have just decreased your chances of ever coming down with cancer.

Wife Has "Female Pattern Baldness"

Dear Cathy:

I met this lady, who is 55 years old, and instantly fell in love with her. Soon afterwards, we were married. However, it bothers me that she doesn't have any hair.

The first time she took her wig off, it turned me off that she was bald underneath. Is there anything that she can do to grow her hair back? *Bald Female Mate, Washington, DC*

Dear Bald Female Mate:

While classic baldness has always been associated with men, what has become increasingly more common today is "female pattern baldness" or "female pattern hair loss."

According to the latest experts, 5 out of 10 women who constantly wear hair pieces, weaves, wigs, scarves, and hats are suffering from "female pattern baldness."

Losing your hair can be devastating for any

woman. It can cause any normal healthy woman to suffer some type of mental anguish or depression.

Hair weaving, hairpieces, or a change in hairstyle, may disguise hair loss and improve her appearance, until she can grow your hair back.

Many women are misdiagnosed with Alopecia by dermatologists, who will tell them to get on "Female Minoxidil" or "Female Rogaine," which causes heart attacks. Just remember that all medications have side effects.

Alopecia is the medical term for excessive or abnormal hair loss. There are different kinds of Alopecia. Female Alopecia is caused by low estrogen levels and results in hair loss.

Most women notice their hair thinning in their 50s or 60s, but it can happen at any age, even during teenage years and for a variety of reasons. Older women may experience this, as can younger women who have low estrogen levels.

Living in a dry climate can also cause your hair to become humid and dry out, so the weather do make a difference in how your hair looks and feel.

Doing too many of the wrong things can not only harm her hair and scalp, and prevent it from looking its best, but it can also cause severe damage.

This will be the time for her to eat a good natural and alkaline diet, especially green and antioxidant foods, and drink alkaline water.

The more alkaline her body is, the quicker and healthier her hair will grow back. Also protein is important for her hair growth. However, just make sure she eats the right type of protein.

Mineral and vitamin deficiencies can cause hair loss, so Omega 3s and other hair supplements are needed to maintain a healthy head of hair.

Chronic dehydration also cause hair loss. Over 75 of people are chronically dehydrated in this country. If she craves salt, she is probably dehydrated. If her lips turns dark, she is probably dehydrated. If she ever get dizzy, again, she might be dehydrated.

People can die from dehydration, so she needs to drink enough water everyday. The best water is Alkaline water, then pure/purified, then distilled water.

I would stay away from Spring water, which automatically causes dehydration and other health issues.

Fighting Off Depression

Dear Cathy:

My wife and I have been married for 25 years and are in our middle 50s. We have a great sex life, when my wife is not going in and out of depression. What can I do to help my wife?
Fighting Off Depression, Michigan

Dear Fighting Off Depression:

This is nothing new because many women today are fighting off depression, so don't think this is only happening to your wife.

What you need to understand is that the number one issue that women face today in most workplaces is depression, but there are a few things you can do.

You still will need to make appointments for exercising because exercising releases endorphins, which makes your brain feel good. So it will be important to keep exercising on both of your schedules.

The brain is involved in everything you do, how you think, feel, act and interact with others. When your brain works right, you work right.

So therefore, she needs to eat good brain foods, especially green foods because green foods releases serotonin, which makes your brain feel good.

The depression supplements are Vitamin D3 for your mood and Omega 3 Flaxseed and Fish Oil Supplements for your brain.

However, all women should take a Multivitamin for women, which will help with PMS and Menopause, and they should get at least 20 minutes of sunlight everyday.

Many people today are overwhelmed because of the toxic world we live in. The Genetically Modified (GM) foods (processed foods) today causes all types of brain issues including depression.

Eating nutrient-dense foods, taking the right supplements for depression, engaging in a regular exercise program, along with getting plenty of rest and sunlight, will be key to her becoming her old self again.

If this doesn't work, she might need to seek out professional help by working with psychologists, psychiatrists or mental health specialists, but try these natural remedies first.

Painful Menstrual Cramps

Dear Cathy:

I know most men don't write in about women's issues, but I really want to do what I can to help my wife, who is the love of my life.

I did not grow up with any sisters and we never had daughters, so I don't know a lot about women's issues.
My wife is 51 and still have periods. She experiences heavy menstrual cycles and painful cramps every month.

She usually have to take one or two days off from work during this time. She also craves chocolate during this time.

Is there anything that she can do naturally to

help ease the cramps and pain, and slow down the bleeding? *Heavy Cramps, New York*

Dear Heavy Cramps:

First of all you need to understand that many women and young girls, also experiences painful menstrual cramps, along with heavy bleeding, which is caused by their diets, especially if they eat toxic GMO processed foods.

The foods have no nutritional value and also causes infertility in women and sterility in men. Until she goes natural and start eating foods in as natural forms as possible, she will continue to experience these symptoms.

These symptoms can lead to fatigue, anemia, shortness of breath and other health issues including cancer.

Periods are considered heavy if there is enough blood to soak a pad or tampon, every hour for several consecutive hours.

Other symptoms could include nighttime bleeding, that requires getting up to change pads or tampons, passing large blood clots during menstruation, and a period that last longer than 7 days.

If she is craving chocolate, it's because she is really craving magnesium. So along with taking a daily Multivitamin for women, she needs to add Vitamin D3 for mood, and Calcium and Magnesium supplements to her diet.

Taking all three of these supplements together works best, and will give her some of the vital nutrients that she is missing.

Sitting in a warm bath or using a hot water bottle can help ease menstrual cramps, but she should be careful taking any over-the-counter pain medication, which can damage her liver.

Unbearable Hot Flashes

Dear Cathy:

I am in my 50s and I have been going through the change. I am experiencing the most unbearable hot flashes, that I ever thought possible.

During the day, no matter what I am doing, I just break out in sweats and this has been really embarrassing for me at work.

At nighttime, the hot flashes have kept my husband and me from getting a good night's sleep, and of course it has also interrupted our sex life.

What really causes hot flashes and is there anything that can be done to eliminate them? *Unbearable Hot Flashes, Washington, D.C.*

Dear Unbearable Hot Flashes:

By the time a women go through the change of life, her body will experience many hormonal changes. These changes might not only cause an interruption in her sleep pattern, but her sex life also.

Many women know very little about going through the change of life or menopause. I suggest you read several books to find out more about the different changes that will be taking place in your body.

First of all you need to understand that not all women have issues with hot flashes. The number one reason that most women experience hot flashes is probably because of their diets, because you are indeed what you eat.

You will experience symptoms of hot flashes if you eat GMO processed foods (any foods in packages, bags, cans, jars, etc. – foods that have been altered).

Remember that all beef and chicken today are fed "Bovine Growth Hormones," which are steroids to make the beef produce more milk and cause the chickens to become larger.

So to stop the hot flashes, you need to clean up your diet and stop eating beef, chicken, eggs, drinking milk and eating other dairy products. So only eat grass-fed beef.

Even white bread, pasta, rice, potatoes, corn and other high-carb foods can also contribute to cycles of moodiness and fatigue, so stop eating all processed foods.

A woman can take a little more control over the consequences of her symptoms by eating better, exercising and getting plenty of sleep.

I recommend you read these two books *"Eat Right 4 Your (Blood) Type,"* which contains a list of foods to eat, and also read my health book *"How To Take Control of Your Own Life: A Self-Help Guide To Becoming Healthier Over the Next*

30 Days" – available as an e-book and paperback at www.www.AngelsPress.com.

Hysterectomy Ends Sex Life

Dear Cathy:

My wife is 53 years old and up until now, we have enjoyed an active sex life. However, after having an hysterectomy, she has lost the desire to enjoy sex, so what can we do? *Lost Desire, Missouri*

Dear Lost Desire:

There are two types of hysterectomies, a "partial" and a "complete" (or total) hysterectomy. In the past there have been a lot of studies conducted and OB/GYN doctors do give women hysterectomies, unnecessarily, especially women of color.

So women should never allow a doctor to remove her eggs completely, when they receive a hysterectomy.

Keep at least one egg because if they give you a COMPLETE or TOTAL hysterectomy, you will be at risk for Heart Disease, Alzheimer's, and Osteoporosis.

This could also be why many nursing homes today are filled with Alzheimer's patients because of how they use to give hysterectomies, unnecessarily, years earlier. They are even calling Alzheimer's *"Type 3 Diabetes."*

If she had a complete hysterectomy, she will be at risk for Osteoporosis, so she needs to keep up with her yearly bone density tests, while eating a natural diet, exercising and getting plenty of rest. Strength training for her bones will also be important.

Dairy products can actually cause an acidic environment to exist in your body and weaken your bones. Sicknesses and diseases thrives in acidic environments in your body.

Therefore, she needs to eat a natural diet, especially foods for her blood type, and get off all dairy products, while maintaining an alkaline diet and lifestyle.

Along with her daily Multivitamin for women, she should be taking Vitamin D3, with

Magnesium and Calcium, Omega 3 Fish Oil and Flaxseed Oil Supplements.

Every woman is different when it comes to a hysterectomy, and just because one woman experiences a low sexual drive after a partial or complete hysterectomy, doesn't mean all women will.

The key to an active sex life is your diet, including vitamin and mineral supplements, exercising and getting plenty of rest. So she need to look at all of these factors first, and weigh all her options, before thinking her sex life is over.

Treat Husband for Yeast Infection

Dear Cathy:

Sometimes I get yeast infections back to back. This has happened most of my active sex life. Even though I get treated from the doctor with a prescription and cream, the infections always come back in the next few weeks or months.

Should my husband also be treated for these infections, to make sure we are not passing it back and forth to each other? *Continuous Yeast Infections, Iowa*

Dear Continuous Yeast Infections:

Yeast is inside all of us. It normally resides in the intestinal tract, mouth, throat and genitals. Yeast can burrow holes in the intestinal tract, enter the blood stream and then make its way into any organ in the body.

To make matters worse, yeast can discharge over 70 different toxins into your body. So yeast is a very common issue with many people, especially today.

First of all you need to get checked to make sure the infections are just yeast infections, so go to the doctor to find this out.

Once you figure this out, you need to know upfront that this is the same issue that many women have today with "vaginal yeast infections."

These can be reoccurring, especially if you don't get rid of the reason for it in the first place. Most of these infections in women, will flare up every time they end up on antibodies.

Most doctors, or those that really care about their patients, know when they give you a prescription for antibodies, to also give you one for the yeast infection that it will cause.

Some doctors don't do this because the pharmaceutical industry is big business, and many want you to end up back at the doctor's office.

Though yeast infections are more common in women, anyone can get one. It's possible for a man to get a genital yeast infection, if he has unprotected sexual intercourse with a partner, who has a genital yeast infection.

However, if a woman has a yeast infection, it doesn't mean that a man will get it too. Sexual transmission of yeast infections is uncommon.

Signs and symptoms of a male yeast infection include a reddish rash, itching or burning at the tip of the penis. Most male yeast infections are easily treated with over-the-counter antifungal treatments, such as Monistat cream (yes, men can use it too).

Apply the medication or cream directly to the affected skin twice daily for a week. If the rash doesn't go away, or if it recurs frequently, consult your doctor.

In women, a yeast infection causes itching or soreness in the vagina, and sometimes causes pain or burning when you urinate or have sex.

Some women also have a thick, clumpy, white discharge, that has no odor and looks a little like cottage cheese.

These infections are very common. Although, they can bother you a lot, they are not usually serious. And treatment is simple, which is over-the-counter Monistat cream.

Since these infections are so common, they have now made a 1 day pill and a 3 day cream, but I would stick with using the cream for 7 days, once or twice daily, especially at nighttime. Once a day for 7 days at nighttime should get rid of any yeast infection.

Once you start eating a more natural diet, clean up your inside environment by using natural products to clean with and to apply to your skin, and engage in regular detoxifications, including a colon, liver, kidney and a heavy metal detox, your yeast infections should go away and never return.

However, a yeast infection will return if a woman go back on antibodies or other medications that automatically causes yeast infections.

If you and your partner both have symptoms of genital yeast infections, it's important that you both be treated. Otherwise, you may keep reinfecting each other.

Also, it's generally recommended that you refrain from sexual contact until all signs and symptoms of the infection are gone.

Controlling Outbreaks of Herpes, Shingles, and Urinary Tract Infections

Dear Cathy:

I contacted herpes years ago from my first husband and now I have been made to suffer this disease for years.

I also suffer from shingles and Urinary Tract Infections (UTIs) and heard they all are closely related to having a yeast overgrowth.

Is there anything that I can do to keep down these infections and outbreaks? *Outbreaks, Virginia*

Dear Outbreaks:

Certainly yeast can play a role in the outbreaks of herpes, shingles and Urinary Tract Infections (UTIs), and it is mainly caused by your diet.

Even though yeast infections are not serious, these infections or a yeast build-up in your body, may play a role in just about any mental health condition, or chronic illness you can think of including herpes, shingles and a UTI.

Herpes is an STD that will be in your body forever, but if you take the steps I am mentioning today, you should very seldom if ever, have an outbreak. As long as you don't have an outbreak, then your mate cannot catch it from you.

At one point shingles mostly occurred in older people, but now men and women in their early 40s are dealing with shingles, because they are eating toxic GMO foods and living in a toxic inside environment.

Many women have Urinary Tract Infections (UTIs) because of the way they are made down there. The tube that transports urine from the bladder to the outside of the body is located close to the anus, and that is why we teach little girls to wipe from the front to back, otherwise they can infect themselves.

Food allergies also mimics Urinary Tract Infections, so many times when it feels like you have a UTI, it could just be food allergies, so try to figure out which foods you are allergic to.

Keep in mind that if you eat GMO processed foods, it causes all of these outbreaks to run out of control. So the goal is to transition to a more natural diet and eat foods in as natural forms as possible -- juiced, steamed, or blended, with very little cooking.

Stress in your body from having an "acidic body" from eating processed foods (foods in boxes, packages, jars, cans – or any foods that have been altered) can also cause these outbreaks to run out of control.

Remember disease and sickness cannot exist in an "alkaline body." If you have an "acidic body," you are moving closer to sickness, disease and death.

However, if you have an "alkaline body," you are moving toward living a healthy, energetic life, a life full of vitality.

So how do you make your body alkaline? You eat green foods, the darker the greens the better, which builds your body and keeps it alkaline.

You eat antioxidants, the blue, purple, yellow, red and orange foods in as natural forms as possible -- juiced, steamed, or blended. Eat foods for your blood type, while drinking the best water, which is alkaline water.

Once you start eating a more natural and holistic diet, clean up your inside environment by using natural products to clean with and to put on your body, engage in regular detoxifications for your colon, liver and kidneys, and a heavy metal detox, you should very seldom, or if ever again, have an outbreak of herpes, shingles or an Urinary Tract Infection.

Viagra Side Effects

Dear Cathy:

I almost took Viagra this past Valentine's Day. I am 50 years old and in pretty good shape. I have never been on any type of medication, but I have been impotent for quite a while.

Do you think it will be okay to take a Viagra pill

sometimes or on special occasions? *Need To Satisfy My Mate, California*

Dear Need To Satisfy My Mate:

No, it's never okay to take any type of medication. All medications have a side effect. All medications, even antidepressants causes depression, so I would not risk it at all.

If you are in pretty good shape and would like to maintain that, then introducing any type of medication, whether it is over-the-counter or prescribed, could literally send your body into shock.

The side effects of taking Viagra is vision loss, hearing loss, and heart attacks. Reactions from medications are either mild or acute, so you never know how your body will react.

Even if you take the pill just once, it can cause any of these reactions. Also it might take you hours to come down from the effects of taking Viagra, and you might end up in the emergency room or worse.

You can even rupture your penis causing excessive bleeding and pain. Your penis can even split straight down the middle, especially if you take too many pills, so understand that Viagra pills are not candy.

There could be a lot of reasons that you are impotent, so you need to get to the root of what is happening to your body.

Go to the doctor and get checked for Erectile Dysfunction (ED), and make sure the doctor check your testosterone level, along with your prostate.

However, the problem could just be your diet, especially if you are eating GMO processed foods, or any foods that have been altered (foods in cans, jars, boxes, packages, etc.).

Every processed food today contain Genetically Modified Organisms (GMOs), which causes infertility in women and sterility in men.

The key to having a strong sex life is found in most holistic and natural communities, if and only if you choose to live a natural and holistic lifestyle.

Health and wholefood stores, located in every community, have supplements that all men (and women) need to maintain a good sex life.

Supplements Raises Sexual Desires

Dear Cathy:

We are in our 50s. I know there are herbs and supplements, which will raise our sex drive. Since my husband and I are not on any medications, we plan on eating a good diet and taking these supplements on a regular basic.

What are some of these supplements that we can take to have a more proactive sex life, as we age gracefully? *Sex Supplements, Maine*

Dear Sex Supplements:

Ginseng is good for your sex life, but not all blood types can take ginseng because it can raise your blood pressure, so read the book *"Eat Right 4 Your Type."*

If you take ginseng, you should get off of it after two weeks, so it will be more powerful, when you go back on it in another two weeks.

Zinc is a good supplement, especially for men with ED or who is impotent. Vitamin E is known as the "Sex Vitamin" in the world of nutrients because it increases the libido for both sexes, and heightens desire, sensitivity and longevity.

Vitamin E (like Vitamin C) is an antioxidant supplement, and antioxidant supplements or antioxidant foods (the fresh, raw and organic blue, purple, red, orange and yellow foods), are the foods that helps keep you healthier by regenerating new cells and increasing longevity.

Ginkgo Biloba and Vitamin E are blood thinners, which are good for men with ED, because it helps with circulation down there.

However, you need to avoid both of these if you are on any type of "over-the-counter" or "prescribed" medication because these are blood thinners, which can have a negative reaction to other supplements or medications.

If you end up in the emergency room or is scheduled for any type of surgery, you need to inform the doctor right away that you are on these herbs and supplements, otherwise, you can bleed out from a wound or operation.

You don't have to take Vitamin E or Gingko Biloba every day for it to be effective, so think about taking the herb every 3 or 4 days, and it still should be able to help you spice up your love life.

Seeking Sexual Activity Through Diet

Dear Cathy:

My husband and I are both retired. We conduct a lot of research and as we age, we wanted to keep eating foods, that might give us a better sex drive.

So which foods should we eat to make us have a better and stronger sex drive, as we age? *Better Sex Drive, North Carolina*

Dear Better Sex Drive:

Eating the right foods will give you longer lasting energy, especially during any type of sexual activity.

Therefore, most couples should eat foods for their blood type, which will give them tons of energy and vitality, so buy the book *"Eat Right 4 Your (Blood) Type"* and maintain a holistic and natural lifestyle.

You can also eat foods containing Vitamin E (The Sex Vitamin), foods containing zinc and citrus fruits, however, I would not eat any of these foods unless they are the foods that are located on your blood type list, in the blood type book mentioned.

Sweet potatoes, raspberries, alfalfa sprouts, carrots and most nuts are just some of the foods which contains Vitamin E. These foods should be consumed 2 to 3 hours before sexual activity, according to many sexual experts.

All processed foods contains GMO corn and soybeans and most people are allergic to corn. When people are allergic to foods, they don't necessarily have to break out in red spots, instead they will feel weak, sluggish or run-down, or just want to go to sleep.

I call these "Good Night Foods" and this is why a lot of people fall asleep at work at their desks, especially after lunch, and in front of the TV after their evening meal, which can cause frustration in any marriage.

Usually your allergic reaction might come as some type of sinus or congestion issue, where fluids builds up. However, it can also be headaches or body aches.

Monitor yourself for up to 72 hours after you eat, to see if you are eating foods you are allergic to. Usually you will have a symptom in 15 to 30 minutes.

Just some of these "Good Night Foods" include chocolate, eggs, dairy products and fried foods. These are also called "mucus-producing foods," which causes inflammation in your body, and causes your body to swell up with fluids on the insides.

Every major disease is associated with inflammation, so to keep it under control, make sure you take Omega 3 Flaxseed and Fish Oil Supplements, while you eat Omega 3 foods, if these foods are on your blood type list.

Healthier Enough for Sex

Dear Cathy:

My husband and I are both in our middle 50s and feel energetic and sexually stimulated most of the time. In other words, we have a nice sex life.

We are not on any medications and we go to a doctor every six months for checkups. We try to eat right, drink good water, exercise and get plenty of rest.

We also use natural cleaning products for our home, put natural products on our bodies and engage in regular detoxification programs. But how can we tell if we are really healthy enough for a long sex life? *Healthy in Chicago*

Dear Healthy:

As long as you are not on any medications and you are keeping your important numbers (cholesterol, blood glucose, blood pressure, triglycerides, waist size (under 40 for men and under 35 inches for women)) in range, then you are fairly healthy and should be able to continue to have a great sex life.

Other ways to tell is by visiting a Kinesiologist, who can look at your *'dry'* and *'live'* blood under a microscope called "Live Blood Cell Analysis." They can tell you if a disease is forming in your body by the way your cells look under a microscope.

Because your blood is the pathway to the flesh and tells all, they can look at your blood and tell you what is happening in your body.

It is really not a diagnostic procedure for any specific disease, but they can tell you if a disease is forming in your body, especially diabetes, and if you are receiving enough Omega 3s, or other nutrients in your diet.

It is best used to help determine the optimal diet and most effective supplementation for enzymes, herbs, antioxidants, etc.

If you can't afford this procedure, then buy pH strips and test your first urine and saliva of the day, but remember that the blood is the most telling of all.

The pH of the blood should be 7.365. If your blood is "alkaline" versus being "acidic," then chances are, you are fairly healthy and again should be able to enjoy a long sex life together.

Ending Message To Singles:
I know it will be mostly women reading this book. So my ending message is to all women, especially single women.

I was single for years after a short marriage that produced two gorgeous daughters. I am now in the third act of my life. The first 30 years was the first act and the second 30 years was the second act.

As I turn 60 years old in October 2016, this is the last act of my life and I have to get it right.

Therefore, I am looking forward to all that life has to offer, whether I am single or in a relationship.

Single women need to stop saying that they are going to wait until they get married to travel the world, or wait until they get married to buy their dream home and other luxuries of life, that they truly desire.

If you truly desire to do these things, then don't wait. If you continue to wait for a mate to live your dreams, then you might not never live your dreams.

And don't forget that many times, it will be your mate that will zap your energy and vitality and keep you from living your dreams.

But because you have lived your dreams when your mate shows up in your life, or if you meet him, while you are out there living your dreams, you will be ready for him.

However, what you also need to understand is that sometimes it might be meant for you to travel this world alone -- without a mate. It does not mean that you are not worthy, and that you are not living a worthy life.

I have spoken to tons of disgruntled single women, who have homes. They spend every dime they have on these big, lonely, empty, homes and can't do anything else, but pay the mortgage, keep the lights on, and buy toxic GMO processed foods.

Instead, they need to sell these homes and downsize and get out there and eat good food and have fun. Be courageous and step out on your faith. When you get older, you especially need to downsize.

Stop being in love with things and fall in love with your brains first and eat good brain foods and take brain supplements.

By doing this, it will help you make better decisions in your life, and bring more happiness into your life, especially as you go into your golden years.

So spend money on your insides, instead of your outsides. Once you fall in love with your brains, you will have more options and choices in your life.

Happiness is an inside job and women need to stop making excuses why they can't buy organic foods, which will give them more energy and vitality, while keeping down doctor's visits.

Some women buy all these beautiful things around them, then they have to cry themselves to sleep at night, because they are all alone and just unhappy. They don't have anything else but expensive things around them.

Some spend hours on the phone gossiping, criticizing and complaining or looking at television, when their homes could literally become learning centers, where they can empower themselves and their families to build a new life.

You need to put all that sexual energy into something else -- a hobby, a business or travel. The goal is to figure out your true purpose and get out there and live it before you leave this earth.

Do the things that you were truly put on this earth to do and have fun doing it. Again, nothing is etched in stone in your life.

And never forget that no one can complete you, but you, which means only you can carve out the type of life that you truly desire.

Ending Message to Couples:
I believe there are 4 areas which couples need to build around -- *Love, Communication, Trust* and *Respect.*

There must be *love* in the first place in order for you to be in someone's life; You must be able to *communicate* everyday of your relationship, which means no words should be left unsaid; You must have *trust* that when the both of you get out of bed everyday, the other person will put the other person's needs first - always; and *respect* is very important because once couples start losing respect for each other, everything changes and not for the better.

5 Points To Remember:
There are 5 points that everyone need to understand when it comes to relationships:
-Don't try to commit yourself to a person, who is obviously not ready for you to be in their life. When it is time, it will or won't happen.

-If you are in a relationship where your partner devalues who you are, then move on. Ladies never forget that "one man's loss is another man's treasure," so if you are being mistreated, chances are another man will probably treat you like the queen that you are.

-Guys when you see that woman and you know she is a queen, don't spend an entire lifetime getting with her. Always keep her close and make her a part of your life, before you lose her to another man. If you know that she is special, then other men will know that also.

-Don't put your dreams on hold waiting for the right person to come into your life. Get out there and live your dreams!

-Be grateful for all your life experiences, whether you are walking this earth with a mate or alone. Love every minute of your life!

ABOUT THE AUTHOR

"We Can Sit Back and Watch as the World Goes By or We Can Find Opportunities to Make it Better!"
-Cathy Harris

Cathy Harris is an Empowerment and Motivational Speaker, Advice Columnist, Non-GMO Health and Wellness Expert, Business and Self-Publishing Coach and is the author of over 20 non-fiction books.

She is known as a woman in the business of uplifting and empowering her community and is a wealth of knowledge when it comes to moving forward.

She is an expert on topics such as family and community empowerment, health, youth and adult entrepreneurship, writing and publishing, workplace discrimination (sexism, sexual harassment, sex and race discrimination), whistleblowing, domestic and international traveling, government, law enforcement, politics, media, aging/retirement, beauty/self-esteem – just to name a few.

Cathy is a veteran and lives in Austin. She is available for lectures, seminars, workshops and webinars at http://www.CathyHarrisInternational.com. For more empowerment information, join the mailing list and buy other books by Cathy Harris at www.AngelsPress.com.

CATHY HARRIS
LECTURES, SEMINARS &
WORKSHOPS

http://www.CathyHarrisInternational.com

If you have enjoyed this book and want more assistance on how to move forward, consider attending one of Cathy's lectures, seminars, or workshops.

Lectures, seminars, and workshops are planned for the U.S. and internationally. You can benefit from a half, full, or several days of Cathy's lectures, seminars, or workshops. She will gladly travel to your city and meet with your group.

She is also available for in-home health and business workshops.

Be sure to sign up on her website at:

Angels Press
Cathy Harris, CEO
Speaker, Author, Coach
P.O. Box 19282
Austin, TX 78760
Phone: (512) 909-7365
Website: http://www.angelspress.com
Email: info@angelspress.com

OTHER BOOKS BY CATHY HARRIS

The Cathy Harris Story
The Failure of Homeland In-Security
Flying While Black
Domestic and International Traveler's Survival Guide
Recession Survival Guide
Workplace Survival Guide
Discrimination 101 (Volume I & Volume II)
Police Interactions 101
How To Write A Book
Golden Years
My Hair, My Crown, My Glory
Diabetes 101
Cancer Cures
How To Raise Smart, Talented and Responsible Children
Politics 101
The New CEO
A Woman's Guide to Buying a New or Used Vehicle (Part I & II)
A Self-Help Guide to Empowering Your Family and the Entire Community (Series 1)
A Self-Help Guide to Starting Your Own Business (Series 2)
A Self-Help Guide to Becoming Healthier Over the Next 30 Days (Series 3)

ARTICLES BY CATHY HARRIS

How To Engage in a Complete Detoxification Program
How To Gain Back Your Mental Clarity by Eliminating Heavy Metals
How To Publish a Digital Book (E-book)
How To Gain Funds to Finance Your Business
How To Survive Unemployment
How To Set Up a Legal Defense Fund for False Imprisonment or Wrongful Workplace Termination

3-PART EMPOWERMENT BOOK SERIES
Series 1, 2, 3

How To

TAKE
CONTROL
of Your
OWN
LIFE

Series 1

A Self-Help Guide to
Empowering Your Family
and the Entire Community

CATHY HARRIS

How To

TAKE
CONTROL
of Your
OWN
LIFE

Series 2

A Self-Help Guide to
Starting Your Own
Business

CATHY HARRIS

How To

TAKE
CONTROL
of Your
OWN
LIFE

Series 3

A Self-Help Guide to
Becoming Healthier
over the Next 30 Days

CATHY HARRIS

OTHER POPULAR BOOKS
BY CATHY HARRIS

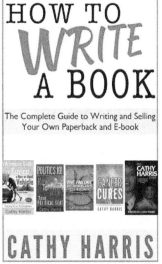

Order at http://www.AngelsPress.com

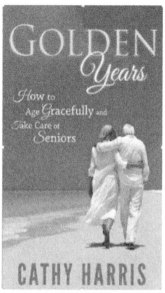

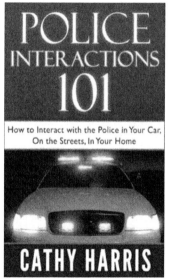

Order at http://www.AngelsPress.com

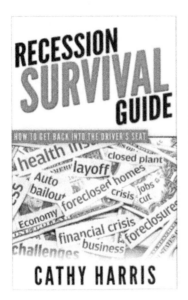

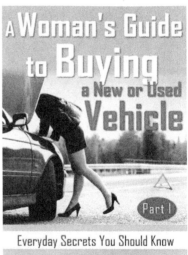

Order at http://www.AngelsPress.com

Printed in Great Britain
by Amazon

64843242R00071